GREAT MINDS OF SCIENCE

The Leakeys
Uncovering the Origins
of Humankind

Margaret Poynter

Enslow Publishers, Inc.

44 Fadem Road	PO Box 38
Box 699	Aldershot
Springfield, NJ 07081	Hants GU12 6BP
USA	UK

Library of Congress Cataloging-in-Publication Data

Poynter, Margaret
    The Leakeys : uncovering the origins of humankind / Margaret Poynter.
      p. cm. — (Great minds of science)
    Includes bibliographical references and index.
    Summary: Profiles the lives of Louis and Mary Leakey and their dedica-
tion to the study of human evolution.
    ISBN 0-89490-788-3
    1. Leakey, L.S.B. (Louis Seymour Bazett), 1903–1972—Juvenile
literature. 2. Leakey, Mary D. (Mary Douglas), 1913–1996—Juvenile
literature. 3. Anthropologists—Kenya—Biography—Juvenile literature.
4. Fossil hominids—Africa, East—Juvenile literature. [1. Leakey, L.S.B.
(Louis Seymour Bazett), 1903–1972. 2. Leakey, Mary D. (Mary Douglas),
1913–1996. 3. Anthropologists.] I. Series.
GN21.L37P69 1997
599.9'092'2–DC21   96-40899
                                         CIP
                                         AC

Printed in the United States of America

10 9 8 7 6 5 4 3 2 1

Illustration Credits: AP/Wide World Photos, pp. 26, 70, 92, 103, 108;
Enslow Publishers, Inc., pp. 6, 49; Leakey Family Collection, pp. 9, 11,
19, 25, 33; Dr. Gilbert H. Grosvenor ©National Geographic Society,
pp. 35, 62, 75, 100; Melville Bell Grosvenor © National Geographic
Society, pp. 56, 66, 82, 96; National Geographic Society, pp. 46, 55,
84; Baron Hugo Van Lawick/National Geographic Society Image
Collection, pp. 23, 41; Volkmar Kurt, Wentzel/National Geographc
Image Collection, p. 73.

Cover Illustration: AP/Wide World Photos (inset); © Elizabeth
DeLaney/Visuals Unlimited.

Contents

The Valley of Bones

IN EAST AFRICA, IN THE COUNTRY OF Kenya, there is a plain. Two million years ago, this plain was covered by a lake. Strange-looking elephants, horses, buffaloes, pigs, apes, and apelike creatures lived near the lake. As time passed, their remains were covered by layers of sand and volcanic ash.

Long ago, an earthquake shook the area. The water was drained from the lake. Later, heavy rains fell. A raging stream cut its way along the ancient shoreline. A chasm, or gorge, was formed. The buried bones were now exposed in the walls of the gorge.

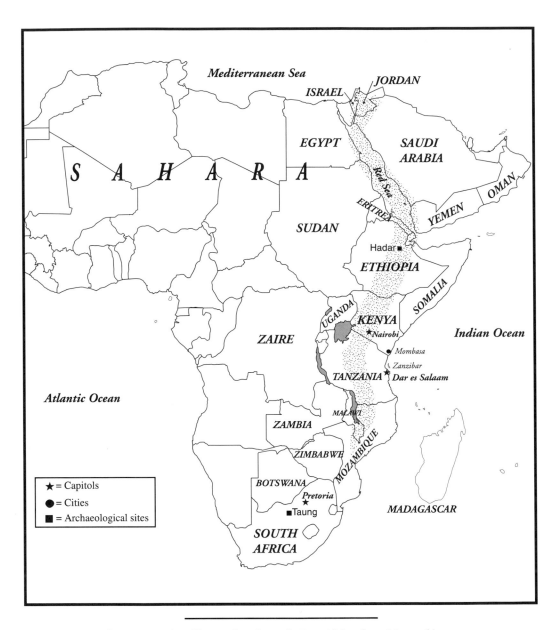

The Great Rift Valley snakes through East Africa from Mozambique to Israel. The Valley contains numerous sites where fossils of early humans are found.

It was here to Olduvai, the Place of Wild Sisal, that Louis and Mary Leakey came in 1935. They were trying to find the answers to two questions: When did our human ancestors first appear on Earth? And where had they appeared? Perhaps the answers lay in the bones of the hominids, the apelike creatures that had lived in Olduvai. Louis believed that most of those creatures had become extinct. Like the dinosaurs, they had died out. He also believed that some of them had not become extinct. They had become the first human beings.

Partial skeletons of these hominids had been found in South Africa. Louis believed that hominids had lived in East Africa before they appeared anywhere else. For over twenty years, the Leakeys labored under the hot sun. The air they breathed was filled with fine black dust. The water they drank was covered with green scum. At night, lions prowled the edge of their camp. Louis and Mary found animal bones. They found stone tools. They did not find any hominid bones, but they continued their search.

On July 17, 1959, Louis was not feeling well. Mary told him to rest while she worked. She chose a layer of land that had been formed more than a million years ago. Here, there were many bone fragments lying on the ground. One of them was partly buried. Mary carefully brushed away the dirt. She uncovered parts of a skull.

She brushed away more dirt. There were parts of two large teeth in the upper jaw. They were not pointed, as apes' teeth are. They were flat, as they were in hominids. Mary rushed back to camp to tell Louis about her discovery. He jumped out of bed, his illness forgotten. If Mary was right, then hominids had lived in East Africa. They had been there before they appeared in South Africa.

Louis felt that one of his dreams was about to come true.

Louis Leakey was an anthropologist. Anthropology is the study of human beings. Mary Leakey was an archaeologist. She studied the tools and artwork of ancient human beings. Both sciences try to answer such questions as: When

The Leakey family poses in front of the mud-walled bungalow where Louis was born. Louis is in his mother's lap. Julia is standing beside them. Gladys is holding Harry Leakey's hand.

and where did humans first appear on Earth? What did they look like? How did they survive? How intelligent were they? How were they different from the apes they resembled?

Louis's father, Harry, and his mother, Mary, were missionaries. With his sisters, Gladys and Julia, they had come to Kenya from England. It was here that Louis was born on August 7, 1903. The native Kikuyu had never seen a white baby. From miles around, they came to look at Louis. They touched him and felt his hair. Some of them spit on him. That was their way of warding off evil spirits.[1] Louis's mother always kept a sponge nearby.

In 1907, Louis's brother, Douglas, was born. All the Leakey children spoke both English and Kikuyu. Louis taught his native friends how to play barefoot soccer. They taught him how to throw a spear and use a war club. At night, they sat around a campfire. Here, the men of the tribe talked about their tribal history and customs. When Louis was thirteen, he was adopted as a junior warrior. How proud he was to be a "white Kikuyu."

Louis's father took his children on walks in the forest. Louis learned the habits of antelopes and wild cats and birds. Every morning, he studied lessons. In his favorite book, which was about the Stone Age people of Britain, he saw pictures of the stone tools they had made. Louis began collecting sharpened pieces of volcanic rock. To him, these rocks were links to the Stone Age people of East Africa. At that time, nothing was known about the early people of Africa.

The Leakeys returned to England in 1919, when Louis was sixteen. The following year, he entered college. He liked studying prehistory, the time when very ancient people lived. Otherwise, he was not happy in college. In Africa, he had been free to walk in the forest whenever he wanted. Now he had to be on time

The Leakey children get their picture taken. Louis sits in front of Gladys, Douglas, and Julia.

for classes. He had to get a pass to go shopping. He had to go to bed at a certain time, even if he was not tired.

In Africa, Louis's Kikuyu friends had looked upon him as their leader. Here, his classmates did not care that he could track animals and build huts. They knew only that he did not know how to swim or play cricket. He talked with a strange accent. Even his walk was different. Louis placed one foot directly in front of the other, as he had done on the narrow African paths.[2]

In 1922, Louis entered Cambridge, a famous English university. Here he had more freedom, but he had only a few friends. He rushed from class to class. His mind was full of thoughts of ancient people. One student said Louis was "overcharged and unbalanced, and unlikely to make good."[3] To attract attention, Louis bragged about how he could cook. He told everyone he could fix a bicycle and hunt wild animals. His bragging made him more unpopular than ever. To quiet him, some boys once locked Louis in a coal bin.[4]

One day in October 1923, Louis was playing rugby. He was accidentally kicked on his head, but he kept playing. He was kicked again. The next morning, he had a bad headache. After ten days of rest, he tried to study, but he could not remember what he read. A doctor told him he had to quit college for a year.

Louis spent the next eight months in Kenya. He dug long ditches. He suffered from malaria and headaches and aching muscles. He fought off mosquitoes, scorpions, snakes, and an angry buffalo. His pet baboon was carried off by a leopard. But he was happy. He was doing something he liked. He was searching for dinosaur bones.

Mary Douglas Nicol was born in London on February 6, 1913. Her father, Erskine Nicol, was an artist. Her mother, Cecilia, had studied art. They both liked to travel. As a young girl, Mary collected seashells along the Italian shore. In Egypt, she saw mummies and the artwork that was buried with them. She saw prehistoric paintings in French caves and ancient tools in French museums. She went through some buckets of dirt from a French cave. There she found blades and scrapers made of flint. As she handled the tools, Mary thought about the people who had made them.[5]

In 1926, the family was staying in a small French village. That spring, Mr. Nicol became ill with cancer. Mary knew he would not live much longer. To forget her grief, she took long walks. She often saw foxes playing together. Sometimes she saw a wild boar. She liked these animals. Watching them brought her a few moments of peace.[6]

After her father's death, Mary and her mother moved back to London, where Mary entered school. She was not happy in school. Her classmates seemed too young for her. She had spoken French for years, but her French teacher gave her low grades. In poetry class, she was told to recite a poem. Instead, she hid in the boiler room. She was then ordered to recite in front of the entire school.[7]

Mary refused. She was told to leave the school

and never to come back. She entered another school. Here, she caused a loud explosion in chemistry class. She was told to leave that school also. Mrs. Nicol decided that Mary did not belong in a regular school. She thought that Mary should become an artist.

Mary had other ideas. She wanted to become an archaeologist. She attended lectures in museums and took classes at a nearby university. She took part in excavations.

She drew pictures of the stone tools that she found. These pictures led to her first meeting with Louis Leakey.

"A Geological Layer Cake"

IN 1926, LOUIS LEAKEY GRADUATED FROM Cambridge. He had earned very high grades. Some people gave him money so he could begin his search for early humans. At that time, many people believed that the first humans had appeared in Asia. A Cambridge professor told Louis to start his search there.

Louis was convinced the first humans had appeared in Africa.[1] By January 1927, he had set up a camp on a farm in Kenya. His native workers lived in tents. Louis lived in a mud hut that used to be a pigsty. At night, hyenas laughed in the distance. Other animals shrieked and howled. Poisonous snakes crawled into the campsite.

Within a few weeks, Louis had dug up several skeletons, some stone tools, and bits of pottery. A farmer named Gamble lived nearby. He told Louis about a large cave on his property. Louis had a hunch that prehistoric people had lived there. When Louis and his team dug fourteen feet down through the cave floor, they found artifacts such as stone tools and pottery. There were also fossils, fragments of human bones. They dug down three more levels and found more such objects. The artifacts in the fourth level had been made over twenty thousand years ago. Louis's hunch had been right.

One day, two young women came to Louis's camp. They were interested in the work he was doing. One of the women was Wilfrida Avern. Louis invited both of them to dinner in his "piggery." There was a python skin drying outside the hut. Bones and native musical instruments hung on the inside walls. Louis cleared bones and stones off the table before they ate. After dinner, the Kikuyu laborers sang native songs.

The next afternoon, Louis took his guests to a burial site. Hippos and flamingos shared a nearby lake. Buffalo and water buck grazed on the plain.[2]

Louis quickly fell in love with Wilfrida, or Frida as she was usually called. Before she left for England, he asked her to marry him. Frida said she would think about it.[3]

Later in 1927, Louis took one hundred crates of artifacts and fossils to England, where he earned money by teaching anthropology. His students crowded into a spare room and sat on packing crates. Louis told them how his hunches told him where to dig. He talked about how he judged the ages of the tools and bones he found. The geology of the site was one clue. Geology is the study of rocks. The earth is made of layers of rock. These layers were formed at different times, called geologic eras. Tools and bones found in one type of rock are probably from one geologic era.

Louis was twenty years old when he went on his first expedition to Tanganyika.

Louis showed the students how to chip flints to make sharp tools. When he ran out of flints, he used a potato.

The next year, Louis returned to Gamble's Cave. This time, Frida went with him as his wife. Louis's brother, Douglas, also made the trip. In the cave itself, Louis found two more human skeletons. In a nearby gully, one of his workers found some stone handaxes. Louis looked at their shape. He studied the geology of the area. It appeared that the tools were between forty thousand and fifty thousand years old.

Louis was eager to tell other scientists what he had found. In 1929, he and Frida went to a meeting in South Africa. Douglas knew that his brother was often too excited about his discoveries. Sometimes Louis thought that certain bones were older than they really were. Douglas told Louis to wait until other experts had looked at them. A Cambridge professor also warned Louis to slow down.

"I entreat you to be careful what you say," he wrote. "It's foolish to try to make a splash."[4]

Louis followed his advice, but it was difficult for him. He was excited about his work. He wanted to share that excitement with every newspaper reporter he met.[5]

Louis never seemed to get tired. Every day, he and his team sifted through tons of dirt. They found every splinter of bone. Like jigsaw puzzle pieces, the bits of bone were matched to each other. Sometimes a partial skeleton was found. The rock surrounding it was left in place. The huge block was encased in plaster. Eight men were needed to carry it back to camp.

As the weeks passed, the team dug to lower levels in the cave. Each day, they found hundreds of tools. They often worked late into the night by lamplight. Louis and Frida numbered and recorded each object before they slept.

Louis's work was the most important part of his life. In 1929, though, he left his dig to help his Kikuyu friends. When the first white settlers arrived in Kenya, some Kikuyu had agreed to lease plots of land to them. The settlers now said they owned the land. The Kikuyu wanted the land back. Louis told some government officials how the Kikuyu felt. Later, some of the Kikuyus received more money for their land. Others received land to replace what they had lost.

It was now time for Louis and Frida to return to England. Here, in April 1931, they became the parents of a baby girl. They named her Priscilla. Frida stayed in England when Louis left for Kenya at the end of June.

Gamble's Cave had been close to roads and shops. The new dig, in Olduvai Gorge, was two hundred miles from any town. Water holes were scarce. There were no roads, only narrow, rutted trails. Dodging obstacles and chugging up steep slopes, the team's trucks crawled along. Snarling lions threatened the intruders.

To Louis, Olduvai was a scientist's paradise,[6] "a geological layer cake."[7]

Its main and side gorges stretched for thirty-five miles. The fossil deposits rose three hundred feet above the sandy floor. Five layers of deposits were visible. Each layer, or bed, had been formed in a different geologic era. Bed

Visitors stand on the rim of Olduvai Gorge. Louis began to dig here because five layers of fossil deposits were visible to his team.

One was at the bottom of the gorge. The fossils embedded there were 2 million years old. The fossils at the top of the gorge, in Bed Five, were twenty thousand years old. As Louis stood in the gorge, he could see succeeding layers of East African history.[8]

The next day, Louis was up at dawn. All day, he climbed cliffs. He crawled in and out of gullies. When he found a stone handaxe, he was "nearly mad with delight."[9] Within four days, his team had found twenty-seven more handaxes. Within two weeks, they had found the bones of ancient elephants, crocodiles, and a giant antelope. One day, they found the skeleton of a hippopotamus. Nearby, there were many handaxes. It appeared that a tribe of hunters had eaten the animal.

In September, Frida and Priscilla arrived in Africa. Louis wanted them to come to Olduvai. Frida did not want her baby to live near wild animals.[10] She moved into a house next door to Louis's parents. Three days later, Louis returned to Olduvai. There he found the skeleton of an elephantlike creature. Its bones were in the lowest level of a small gorge. The location showed it must have lived 2 million years ago.

By November, the camp's main water hole had dried up. It was time to leave. By then, Louis had found stone tools in each of the five beds. The tools from the bottom bed were just lumps of rock with a rough cutting edge. They

Louis used this truck on his first trip to Olduvai in 1931. He is standing on the running board.

were the oldest tools in the world. The tools in the upper levels had better designs.

By the spring of 1932, Louis was working in Kanam, three miles west of Olduvai. It was the rainy season. Crawling through the mud, Louis found the jaw of an extinct pig. He also found the bones of the same elephantlike creature he had found in Olduvai. At the same time, a worker found some hominid teeth. Later he found a hominid jaw nearby.

Louis was delighted. The hominid must have lived at the same time as those ancient creatures. The stone tools found in the area were from the same era. Louis was certain it was the "oldest known human fragment yet found on the African continent."[11] Perhaps it was the oldest trace of a hominid ever found in the world.

Louis marked the spot with four iron pegs set in concrete. He also took some pictures of the site, but his camera failed. A friend later took another picture. He gave the picture to Louis.

Louis also discovered these human skull fragments at Kanjera during his 1932 expedition.

"I'm not sure that this is the exact spot," he said.

Louis was not interested in details. "Near enough," he replied.[12]

Louis believed he had enough proof to convince other experts. His article about the Kanam jaw was published two months later. Louis brought the jaw to England. A group of scientists looked at it. All but one said that it was only five hundred thousand years old. A geologist, Percy Boswell, needed more proof of the jaw's age. He wanted to see the site for himself.

Meanwhile, Louis was giving lectures about his work in Africa. Mary Nicol went to one of those lectures. Louis had already seen some of her artwork. He asked her to do some drawings for his next book. Mary was eager to work with an anthropologist.

At this time, Frida was expecting their second child. The marriage, however, was failing. Frida wanted to live in England. Louis's happiness lay in the bush country of Africa.

3

Learning a Lesson

AFTER MEETING MARY, LOUIS RETURNED to Africa. Mary went to southern England to dig for artifacts. In her spare time, she drew pictures of handaxes for Louis's book *Adam's Ancestors*.

In the summer of 1933, there was a meeting of archaeologists in London. Mary and Louis went to that meeting. There they saw each other every day. In December, Louis's son, Colin, was born. A month later, Frida and Louis separated. Mary had always admired Louis. When he asked her to marry him, she knew she loved him.[1]

At this time, Mary had to stay in southern England to finish her work. Louis had to go back to Africa. Three months later, in January 1935, Percy Boswell was on his way to Kenya. Louis went to Kanam. He had been gone for three years. Everything looked different. Heavy rains had eroded the area. Many trees had been cut down. Louis could not find the site where he had found the jaw. The pegs marking it were gone. Native fishermen had taken them to make harpoons.

Louis looked at the picture his friend had taken. It did not look like the place where he had found the jaw. Louis was dismayed.[2]

Percy Boswell arrived one week later. Louis told him what had happened. He had no evidence to prove the jaw's age. Boswell was angry that he had come on a "wild goose chase."[3] He later wrote an article attacking Louis and his work at Kanam. Newspapers around the world printed the story. Louis had learned a lesson. He should have drawn an exact map of the site. He should have made sure his camera was working. He should have had a geologist examine the area. Now it was too late. His reputation had been damaged.

After this incident, Louis always carried two cameras. He checked and rechecked his evidence. He was still always in a rush, though. He scribbled notes on scraps of paper. When he needed them, he could not find them.

While Boswell was in Kanam, Mary was on her way to Africa. Louis met her at the airport. After picking up a friend, they headed toward Olduvai. Two days later, they reached the foot of a volcano. It was the middle of the rainy season. The road up the volcano's side was covered with sticky black mud. Their car became stuck several times. Each time, they had to unload their luggage and push the car. They then walked back to get their luggage. It was still raining when they reached the top of the volcano. That night they slept on a canvas tarp spread on the wet ground.[4]

The next morning, the sky was clear. Mary stood on the rim of the volcano. The Serengeti plain lay before her. Moving across its grassy surface were thousands of animals. Wildebeests, zebras, giraffes, gazelles, and impalas were migrating. Mary later wrote that "Africa cast its spell" on her.[5]

The parched soil at Olduvai had already soaked up the rainwater. Before long, the green grass on the plain was turning brown. During the day, everyone became covered with fine white dust. The water the team had brought had to be rationed. When it was gone, they had to use the water from smelly pools. The food supply grew short. They had only canned sardines, apricot jam, and cornmeal to eat.[6]

Louis had learned a lesson from his Kanam experience. He tried not to be in such a hurry. After all, the treasures at Olduvai had been buried for as much as 2 million years. A few more weeks or months would not make any difference. Louis mapped more than a hundred miles of possible digging sites. Only then did he start excavating.

Meanwhile, Mary was learning about life in the wild. One day, she and Louis were walking along a dry streambed. They rounded a curve and faced a rhinoceros. On another day, Mary almost stumbled over a sleeping lion. She was lucky. The lion was as frightened as she was. They ran in opposite directions.[7]

Three months passed. During that time, the team found many traces of ancient plants and animals. They also found scores of handaxes. Mary found two small pieces of human skull. No one found any bones of very early hominids.

By this time, they were almost out of supplies. It was time for Louis to return to England to raise more money. He and Mary arrived in London in September 1936. The next month, Frida divorced Louis. Mary and Louis were married on Christmas Eve. Three weeks later, they were on their way back to Kenya. Louis had made some money by giving lectures. He was also being paid to write a history of the Kikuyu people.

Louis had already written one book about the Kenyan natives. His friendship with them angered many white settlers. They said he was a

Louis and Mary pose with the bones of a prehistoric elephant on their first expedition together in 1935. Sitting on the left is Peter Kent, a student who served as the expedition's geologist.

traitor to his own race. The natives said that Louis was familiar with their point of view.[8] Many of them hoped he could bring understanding between them and the settlers.[9]

After a tribal meeting, Louis was given permission to write his new book. It would be the most complete record of a tribe that had ever been written. Every day, Louis met with the older Kikuyu. He asked them questions and wrote down their answers. By the end of May, he had completed five hundred pages.

While Louis worked on his book, Mary dug in

a nearby cave. Her work was interrupted when she caught pneumonia. The doctors thought she was going to die. For many days and nights, Louis sat by her hospital bed. Her mother flew from England to be with her. Mary surprised everyone. By August, she had completely recovered.

At this time, Louis had finished his interviews with most of the Kikuyu. He and Mary and their crew moved to Hyrax Hill. Below the hill spread the Rift Valley. Here there was a lake from which more than a million flamingos drank at certain times of the year.[10]

As they set up camp, clouds of mosquitoes filled the air. A cobra lived on the roof of the Leakeys' grass hut. The snake finally left. The mosquitoes stayed.[11]

While Louis wrote, Mary excavated a mound of big stones. She uncovered nineteen human skeletons. The objects buried with them told her these people had lived three hundred years ago. Other sites held artifacts that were two thousand

Louis grew up among the Kikuyu people, and he and the tribe held a mutual respect. Louis and Mary often gave free medical care to the natives.

years old. The Leakeys' small dwelling was over-flowing with her discoveries.

The local white settlers were surprised by Mary's discoveries. They had believed that not much had happened in Africa before Europeans arrived. Mary invited people to look at her dig.

The first day, four hundred visitors arrived. Some of them gave her money so she could continue her work.

One visitor told Mary about a cave in a forest near her farm. At that site, Mary and Louis found eighty human skeletons as well as animal skins, baskets, fabrics, and jewelry. Mary excavated the artifacts. Louis excavated and preserved the bones. Each day, they were up at dawn. They did not stop work until long after dark.

By the time Louis finished his book, the money he had received for it was gone. Finding a job was not easy. It was 1939, and World War II was beginning. Italy had already invaded Ethiopia, in northern Africa. The Kenyan government did not have any money to spend on archaeology. It was needed for defense. There were jobs in England, but Louis did not want to leave Kenya.

He was finally hired by the British government as a member of the Special Branch. Most of the native people of Kenya did not know that northern Africa was in danger from Italy and

Germany. They did not know why England might have to fight those countries. Louis's job was to explain why England needed their help.

He was also supposed to find out if the natives were planning any uprisings. Many of them hated the British, who controlled their government. They wanted their country to be free. Louis understood how they felt. But he knew that violence was not the answer to their problems.

In September, England declared war on Germany. Louis was put to work taking guns to Ethiopia. The guns were used to defend Ethiopia against the Italian invaders. At the same time, Louis never forgot that he was a scientist. Whenever he had time, he darted off to inspect a possible digging site.

4

"A Bit of a Maverick"

IN THE SPRING OF 1940, MARY AND LOUIS moved to Nairobi, where they were given space in the Coryndon Museum. They now had a place to store the objects they found.

They were also given a rundown house in which to live. On November 4, their son, Jonathan, was born. When he was a few weeks old, thousands of army ants attacked him. His screams brought Louis and Mary running to his room.

Ants were not the only insects to invade the house. Two colonies of bees lived inside its hollow walls. Once the ants fought a two-day war with the bees. The bees won. Mary had to sweep up thousands of dead bugs.[1]

Louis was still doing war work for the British. Whenever he had time, he came back to Nairobi. Sometimes he took care of Jonathan while Mary worked at a digging site. At other times, they took Jonathan and their dogs and drove to a digging site together. They spent five days in Olduvai. They went to Rusinga, an island in Lake Victoria. One Easter morning in 1942, they drove with some friends to a location south of Nairobi where there was a dry lake bed.

Everyone went off in different directions. Within minutes, Louis had found a great number of handaxes. At the same time, Mary and their friends were calling to him. Everyone had found very large handaxes, cleavers, and stone balls. There were so many artifacts that Louis could scarcely believe his eyes.[2]

Louis and Mary could spend only one day at the new site. They returned there in December, just before their daughter, Deborah, was born. Just three months later, in April 1943, Deborah died. Louis and Mary suffered greatly from their loss. In a letter to a friend, Louis wrote about the death: "I have not been touching any of my work."[3]

As spring turned into summer, Mary and Louis slowly overcame their grief. They returned to their busy schedules. Louis worked at his government job all day. After dinner, he worked at the museum. One museum staff member said that Louis always seemed to have a thousand projects going at once. He "scurried around the museum so fast that he almost fell over his own feet."[4]

Mary also put in long hours at the museum. Sometimes she took Jonathan and the dogs and went to an excavation site. In August, she and Louis went back to the dry lake bed. Louis hoped to discover the campsites of early human beings. The sites could hold clues about the way they had lived.

The lake bed was a disappointment. There were no ancient campsites. There were no skeletons. There were just a great number of ancient

*Mary's dogs always went with her to her digs. They protected her from
wild animals. Her pet monkey was just along for the ride.*

tools. Nevertheless, the site became famous. Scientists from all over the world came to see it.

Another trip to Rusinga was much more successful. Louis found a *Proconsul* jaw. The jaw had a full set of teeth on one side. From the jaw, experts could tell how the shoulder blade was constructed. From the shoulder blade, they knew how the front legs were formed. In this way, from only one bone, they could imagine how the entire animal looked. *Proconsul* appeared to be an ancestor of the modern chimpanzee.

By 1943, the Italians had been driven out of East Africa, but another danger had appeared. Japan had joined Italy and Germany in the war. Japanese submarines were patrolling the Kenyan coast. For two years, Louis made trips to the coast. He found African natives who were giving the Japanese food and water. He found others who were telling the Germans about British troop movements.[5]

On December 19, 1944, Mary gave birth to another son, Richard. The next year, the war ended. As a member of the Special Branch,

Louis sometimes investigated murders and robberies. He liked being a detective, but the job did not pay much money. He had never been paid by the museum, but now he became its curator. He was paid only half as much as he could have made as a teacher, but to teach, he would have had to leave Kenya. His heart was in Kenya. So was the work that he loved.

As curator, Louis welcomed all races to the museum. For the first time, Africans and Asians joined whites in viewing the exhibits.

By 1945, it had been eight years since Louis and Mary had been to England. Mary's mother was ill and wanted to see Mary and her sons. In the spring of 1946, Mary decided to visit her.

Louis could not go. He was planning a Pan-African Congress of Prehistory. For ten years, many people had been exploring Africa's past. Many tools and bones had been found in South Africa. *Proconsul* had been found in Rusinga, the Island of Apes. Some of the fossils found there seemed to be from the Miocene period. Those fossils were 20 million years old.

Many experts were changing their minds. Maybe Africa really was the birthplace of modern human beings. The Congress would give them a chance to talk to each other.

Mary's trip to England was not pleasant. The ship was very crowded. Several people were crammed into each cabin. The weather was either very hot or very cold. Richard cried from the pain of an earache. There were still explosive mines in the Red Sea. There was a chance that the ship might strike one and be blown up. Everyone had to be prepared to run to the decks at a moment's notice.

London had changed since Mary had last seen it. During the war, it had been bombed by the Germans. Its buildings were blackened hulks. The streets were filled with rubbish. There were bomb craters everywhere. The people looked tired. It no longer seemed like home to Mary.[6]

When Mary saw her mother, she was even more dismayed. Mrs. Nicol was very ill, and two weeks later, she died. Mary felt very sad. She wished she would have spent more time with her mother.[7]

Mary could not return to Kenya because there was no room on any ship. She was very homesick. One day she took Jonathan and Richard to the zoo. The roaring of the lions made her cry. She begged Louis to come to London.[8]

Louis wanted to be with his family, but planning the Congress took all his time. He hoped its success would help his career. Some people still remembered the Kanam incident. Others said that he should announce his discoveries only in scientific journals. Louis always carried one of his discoveries with him. He showed it to every newspaper reporter he met. Because he liked publicity, he was called "a bit of a maverick" by other scientists. As a result, he often had trouble getting money for his work.[9]

In the end, the Congress gave Louis the chance to be with his family again. He was given money to fly to London to invite scientists to the meeting. He was happy to see Mary and the

Louis holds a bola, which is used to entangle the legs of fleeing animals.

children, but he could not spend much time with them. He had to visit many schools and laboratories. Everywhere he went he carried his *Proconsul* jaw in a tin cookie box lined with cotton. Many people saw it when he appeared on television.

By early October, Louis and Mary were back in Nairobi. They had a lot of work to do before

January 14, 1947. On that date, sixty scientists came to the conference. The first week, there were lectures and discussions. During the second week, Louis took everyone on a tour of his digging sites.

The Pan-African Congress was a great success. It was decided to have such a meeting every four years. Louis was praised for bringing everyone together. He was also praised for his work as an anthropologist. He was no longer called a maverick. He was now known as a dedicated, inspired scientist.

Unlike Louis, Mary had always been quiet about her work. During the conference, she was praised for what she had done. Mary was no longer known only as Louis Leakey's wife. Scientists now knew that she was as dedicated and inspired as her husband.

An Exciting Find

AFTER THE CONGRESS, LOUIS AND MARY were eager to return to Rusinga. Their first trips to this small island had been made in canoes or sailboats. The journey took ten to twelve hours. Once they had to sleep on bags of corn that were crawling with huge cockroaches.

After the Congress, Louis found it easier to get donations for his work. The Kenyan government gave him money. The Royal Society, a British scientific group, also helped. This time, the Leakeys and their dogs traveled to Rusinga in a large motorboat. They arrived in only eight hours.

Eighteen to 20 million years earlier, a volcano had erupted on Rusinga. Ash buried many of the plants and animals living there. Over the centuries, rain and wind uncovered them. Almost every square foot of the island contained fossils. Soon after their arrival, Louis found a *Proconsul* tooth. Just fifty yards away, a worker found a

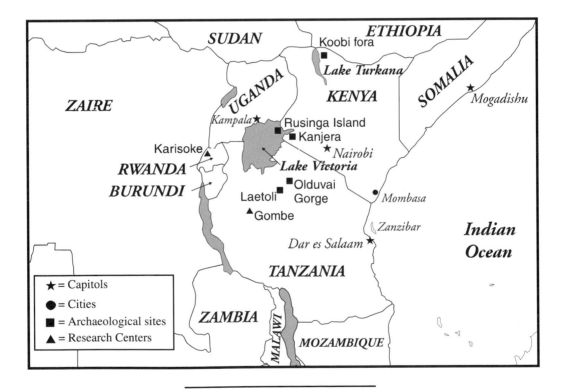

Though the Leakeys lived in Kenya, most of their work was done in Tanzania.

rhino jaw. Over the next few weeks, most of the rhino's skeleton was uncovered.

By the end of November 1947, the team had collected more than thirteen hundred fossils. They included the teeth, upper and lower jaws, and palates of ancient apes. There were ancient elephant, rhino, pig, fish, rodent, insect, and plant fossils. Louis could now imagine what life was like for the apes that had lived on Rusinga.

At this time, an American, Wendell Phillips, was planning a trip to Africa. He also wanted to find traces of early humans. He was going to dig in some of the places that Louis and Mary were exploring. Rusinga was one of those places.

Louis was willing to help Phillips in his search, but he was not willing to share his digging site with him. Louis's British friends heard about Phillips's plans. They also did not want an American working on Rusinga. Louis, an Englishman, had found the site. Louis should be the one to continue the work. A wealthy Englishman sent Louis some money. Even Percy Boswell offered his help.

Louis and Mary went to work with renewed energy. They had a hunch they would soon find something very important. On September 30, 1948, they set up camp at a new location. That morning, as he usually did, Louis fired his shotgun into the lake. The sound frightened crocodiles away. When the echoes died down, Jonathan and Richard could enter the water. They had a five-minute bath before the crocodiles returned.[1]

Richard and Jonathan liked the campsite. The breeze from the lake was cool. There were trees to shade them from the sun. Local children often joined them in their games.

After breakfast, the boys followed their parents as they explored gullies and cliffs. The digging sites were often far from the shore. One day, Louis started to excavate a crocodile skull. Mary was not interested in crocodiles. Walking alone through a crumbly gully, she saw some bone fragments lying on a slope. Above them, there was a tooth.[2]

Using a dental pick, she scratched at the soil.

A few minutes later, she shouted to Louis. He ran to her side. Together, they brushed away the earth. There was an entire *Proconsul* jaw. Then a large part of the skull became visible. Both jaws had a complete set of teeth.

Proconsul was an ape that lived 20 million years ago. The Leakeys thought that it may have been one of man's earliest ancestors. "It was a wildly exciting find," Mary later wrote. "Ours were the first eyes ever to see a *Proconsul* face."[3] Until then, the ape had been known only from its jaws, teeth, and a few limb bones.

For several days, Louis and Mary sifted soil. The work was backbreaking. There was no shade. Flies swarmed around them. Four-year-old Richard spent hours crouched against the wall of the gully. He decided he would never become an archaeologist. He did not want to spend his life "hot, sticky, wishing for shade and swatting at lakeflies."[4]

To Louis and Mary, the hard work was worth the effort. They found all the scraps of bone that belonged to the skull. Later, Mary fitted them together. One square inch of the jaw was in thirty-six fragments. Many pieces were the size of a matchhead.[5] Mary described one of them as "only a crumb of bone."[6] The finished skull was very small. It fit into the palm of her hand. It was as fragile as an eggshell.

To Louis, *Proconsul*'s forehead, eye sockets, and jaw joints appeared "more human in form than apelike."[7] Louis believed it may have been an early ancestor of the first human being. He wanted to take the skull to London himself. But Mary had found it. It was Mary, he decided, who should make the trip.

Meanwhile, Louis sent photographs of the skull to some friends in England who agreed that it was a very important discovery. They sent the news to newspapers and magazines. An airline gave Mary a free trip.

Mary held the carefully packed skull in her lap throughout the long trip. She was still holding it when she stepped from the plane. A mob of reporters greeted her. Most of them were surprised that she had found the skull instead of

Louis. Mary had always gone about her work quietly.

She answered a few of their questions; then she went to Oxford University. She felt great relief as she handed her "precious burden"[8] to Wilfred Le Gros Clark.

Le Gros, as he was known, spent the next two weeks studying the skull. At first, he agreed it was more human than ape. Then he studied it more carefully. Its pointed muzzle and narrow nose opening were monkeylike. Its teeth and jaws were apelike. He decided *Proconsul* was a link between monkeys and apes.

The skull was not what Louis had hoped for, but it was still a lucky find. The story appeared in newspapers and on radio and television around the world. Large crowds visited the British Museum of Natural History to see *Proconsul*. Louis and Mary were famous. They no longer had to worry about getting money to carry on their work.

The excitement about *Proconsul* had another benefit. It caused Wendell Phillips to leave

Philip uses some plants to disguise himself. He is sneaking up on a flock of ducks.

Rusinga. He and his team of experts went to South Africa to try their luck there.

On June 21, 1949, a third son, Philip, joined the Leakey family. As the boys grew older, Louis took them for long nature walks. He pointed out birds and butterflies. He showed them how to chip stones into tools and how to make fire by rubbing sticks. The boys learned how to creep up on animals without being detected.

The Leakey family always had many pets living with them. Besides their dogs, they had wildebeest calves, antelopes, cats, baboons, jackals, field mice, a pony, and little furry hyraxes. At one campsite, two ravens called to Mary when she was late with their breakfast. Sometimes their pet python escaped. They usually found it curled up on a neighbor's porch.

Jonathan liked snakes. He often carried one in a bag under his shirt.

The boys liked these living animals more

Louis spent hours on his knees with his eyes close to the ground. His arms and legs were always bruised and scratched.

than they liked fossils. Richard still did not understand why his parents kept digging up those old bones. One day he was hot and tired and hungry. Louis and Mary were not ready to stop their work. Richard began to whine. "I'm bored," he said.

Louis looked up. "Go find your own bone," he said.[9]

At least now I have something to do, Richard thought. A short distance away, he saw a small bone. With some dental picks and a small brush, he started to dig it out. The bone was larger than he had thought. Soon he saw some teeth. He brushed aside more dirt. He forgot about the heat and the flies. He forgot that he was hungry.

He was so quiet that his father came to see what he was doing. Louis was amazed. Richard had found the first complete jaw of an extinct pig. Louis and Mary finished the excavating. Richard was angry at being pushed aside. Again, he told himself that he would never become an archaeologist.

6

The Olduvai Man

DURING THE LATE 1940s AND EARLY 1950s, the native people of Kenya were becoming restless. They still lived under British rule, and they were not allowed to vote. They could not grow certain crops. Many of them had fought for England during World War II. After the war, they received only a small amount of money. White soldiers were given much more.

British settlers had taken much of the natives' land. The Kikuyu had lost more land than any other people. Louis understood their anger. He had grown up among them. He thought of them as his people.

On the other hand, Louis was a British citizen. He still believed that the natives should solve their problems by peaceful means. In 1949, Louis heard that the Kikuyu were holding secret meetings. They were forming a terrorist group called the Mau Mau. The group was so secret that no one has ever found out what the name Mau Mau means.

Louis did not believe in violence. He was also torn between his British homeland and his adopted homeland. As a result, neither the British nor the Kikuyu trusted him completely. At first, the British governor did not believe him when he reported the Mau Maus' plans.

It was a "tense and frightening" time for Louis and Mary.[1] They had to carry guns to protect themselves. Guards were stationed at their home. Someone loosened a bolt on their car. Luckily, Mary was driving slowly when it came off. At a high speed, she could have been killed.

In 1952, Jomo Kenyatta was arrested. The British believed that Kenyatta was a Mau Mau leader. Louis was the interpreter at Kenyatta's trial. Both the British and the Kikuyu believed that he was not interpreting correctly. Each side believed that Louis was trying to help the other side. Finally, Louis decided to withdraw from the trial. Later, though, he translated some letters and documents. These papers were used to convict Kenyatta.

The conviction did not end the violence. About fifteen thousand Kikuyu continued their battle against the government. Louis helped the British find their hiding places. He knew that most of the Kikuyu people were peace-loving.[2] He believed that the members of the Mau Mau were evil.[3] By helping to defeat them, Louis felt he was helping the rest of the Kikuyu people.[4]

Louis showed his loyalty to the natives by asking the British to make some changes. He wanted them to give back the land they had taken. He wanted the British to build schools for the natives. He wanted the British to pay them higher wages. Most important, he wanted the British to let the natives help run their own government.

As a member of the Special Branch, Louis was busy during the Mau Mau rebellion. He still wrote scientific papers and books. He improved the museum. In 1950, he and Mary organized the second Pan-African Congress of Prehistory.

In 1951, they returned to Olduvai Gorge. Louis was certain that they would find the "Olduvai man," an early human. Every day, they were up at dawn. Louis wore baggy overalls with missing buttons and tennis shoes with holes in the toes. After he suffered a sunstroke, Mary insisted he wear a hat. She would often find him bareheaded. His hat was filled with "some precious find."[5]

Louis was always in a hurry. He was anxious to get things done, then move on to the next site. His excavations were often sloppy. Mary was much more careful. Her excavations were always tidy and clean.

Mary and Louis had already found crude tools in Bed One. Some of them were choppers, small rocks with one edge hammered off. In Bed Two, they had found crude handaxes. In Beds

Ancient people made choppers to crack open bones. Choppers were among the tools that Louis and Mary found in Bed One of Olduvai Gorge.

Three and Four, they had found better types of handaxes. On this trip, they started digging in Bed Two. Louis knew that whoever made those tools had been intelligent. They might even be the first direct ancestors of modern human beings.

By the end of 1952, Louis and Mary had

found the remains of many giant pigs, buffalo, and antelopes in Bed One. The horns of one type of buffalo spanned eight feet. A huge pig had tusks a yard long.

Mixed with the animal fossils were hundreds of stone tools. An ancient tribe must have feasted here. The marrow had been sucked out of some of the animal bones.

When Jonathan and Richard were on vacation, they joined Louis and Mary at Olduvai. Louis showed them which plants were poisonous and which they could eat.[6] He taught them how to identify fossils.[7] They learned to listen for the click of dry pebbles. That sound meant there might be a rhino up ahead.[8]

Mary had always liked cave paintings. One day, she was copying some of these ancient works of art while Louis and the boys looked for other paintings. Philip was only two years old. He lagged behind, calling out, "Poor me. Poor me!"[9]

On another day, the family was returning from viewing rock paintings. Philip was riding on Louis's shoulders. Louis thought he saw a log in the tall grass. He put his foot on top of it. The "log" reared up. Louis jumped back. A python slithered into the forest. The snake was eighteen feet long. It was one of the longest that Louis had ever seen.[10]

During the 1950s, Louis and Mary made several trips to Olduvai. They found animal fossils. They also found three hominid teeth. By this time, Louis and Mary were running short of supplies. In the summer of 1959, Louis went to Nairobi to get some money. While he was there, he met some friends who produced a television show, *On Safari*. The friends wanted to film Louis's next excavation. The cameraman would arrive at Olduvai on July 17.

On that morning, Louis did not feel well. Mary told him to stay in camp. She set off to explore a site in Bed One where Louis had found handaxes. By noon, she had not found anything interesting, and she decided to go back to camp. Then she saw a scrap of bone sticking out from the surface. It looked like part of a skull. She brushed away some dirt. There were parts of two hominid teeth set in a hominid jaw. Now she was certain. She had found a large section of a hominid skull![11]

Mary rushed back to camp. "I've got him!" she called to Louis. "I've got him! I've got him!"[12]

Louis jumped out of bed. He forgot that he was sick. He and Mary sped to the digging site. When Louis saw the fossil, he was still excited, but he was also disappointed.[13] The teeth were not those of a true man. They seemed to be those of an australopithecine, a near-man. Several near-men had been found in South Africa. The age of those fossils was not known.

Some experts believed that near-men were direct ancestors of modern humans. Louis did not. He believed that this species had become extinct. Another type of apelike creature had survived. It was that creature who had become our ancestor.

Louis had not forgotten what had happened at Kanam. He did no more digging until the cameraman arrived. Meanwhile, he was puzzling

Stone tools and fossil bones covered the table in the Leakey's workshop at Olduvai.

over something. It was thought that the near-men had not been smart enough to make tools. Their "Olduvai man" had been found in Bed One. There were also stone tools in Bed One.

Perhaps this really was the skull of a very primitive man. Perhaps their long search was finally over. As soon as the cameraman arrived, Louis and Mary started excavating. During the following nineteen days, they sieved tons of dirt. They found the upper jaw, all the teeth, and the facial bones. They found almost all of the top and back of the skull. Only the lower jaw was missing. Around the skull they found tools and cracked animal bones. Six photographers took pictures of the entire excavation.

Mary spent her mornings digging. Every afternoon she worked on her "jigsaw puzzle." By early August, the puzzle was complete. Their "Dear Boy" had a flat face, wide cheekbones, huge cheek teeth, and hardly any forehead. He had been about eighteen years old when he died. Louis was not sure whether this creature had been an ancestor of the human race. He was convinced, though, that it was a new species. He called it *Zinjanthropus*, the "Man from East Africa." Zinj was packed in a cookie tin. Louis and Mary then closed up camp. The fourth Pan-African Congress would be opening in late August. Louis could hardly wait to show Mary's discovery to the delegates.[14]

Jonny's Child

ON THEIR WAY TO THE CONGRESS, LOUIS and Mary stopped at a museum in Pretoria, South Africa. Here, Louis compared Zinj to some *Australopithecus* skulls. They were alike in many ways, but there were some differences. Zinj had a larger skull and larger teeth. Louis arrived at the Congress bursting with excitement. On opening day, there were three speakers ahead of him. Louis was very nervous. He could barely sit still as he waited his turn.

Finally he could wait no longer. "Can't you hurry it up, Clark?" he whispered loudly to the third speaker. "I've got a very important thing here." When it was his turn, he leaped onto the stage. He placed the skull on the podium, then began his talk. He said that Zinj was different from other near-men. Those other species had died out, but Zinj had survived. He was a bridge, a connecting link between the other near-men and human beings.[1]

After the meeting, other scientists looked at the skull. One of them called its teeth "an enormous set of nutcrackers." Most of them doubted that the "Nutcracker Man" was a new species. Despite their concern, the news flew around the world. "A Stupendous Discovery: The Fossil Skull from Olduvai," read one front-page headline.

Louis continued to believe that Zinj was a new species. He declared that the skull was between five hundred thousand and 1 million years old. A short while later, it was proved to be 1.75 million years old. "Dear Boy," Louis said, was the "oldest known toolmaker ever found anywhere."

Louis set off to speak in crowded lecture halls in England and the United States. One hall was

Louis displays Zinj, or "Nutcracker Man," now classified as Australopithecus boisei. *The bony ridge on top of the skull is called the sagittal crest. This is one feature that separates* Australopithecus *and* Homo.

supposed to seat three hundred people. More than five hundred showed up. Louis pulled Zinj from his wooden box. Next to it he placed the remains of a huge extinct ostrich, hippopotamus, and buffalo. Not a sound came from the audience as he started to speak. When he was through, everyone stood, applauding and cheering.

Sometimes Louis spoke to small groups of students. Seated on a packing crate, he whacked out a tool from a piece of flint. He used the tool to crack open a cowbone. He then sucked the marrow from the bone, as ancient people had done.

Louis often talked about the hunting skills he had learned as a boy. Those same skills, he said, were probably used by our ancestors.

Louis liked being in front of an audience. Mary did not. She was happy to stay behind and prepare for the next trip to Olduvai. The money from Louis's lectures would be enough to pay for everything they needed. The grants they would soon receive would pay for many more trips.

The Leakeys' constant worry about money was gone. Their quiet times exploring Olduvai were also gone. They were suddenly famous.

In February 1960, Louis and Mary started excavating the site in which they had found Zinj. Louis could work only on weekends and holidays. Most of his time was spent at the Coryndon Museum. Every day, there were piles of letters to answer. The telephone rang constantly. Exhibits had to be arranged. People lined up at his door with questions and requests for help. Some of them were Kikuyu. Louis was a "big man," in their view. He was supposed to give advice and money. He never turned anyone down.

Mary had full charge of the work at Olduvai. Nineteen-year-old Jonathan became camp manager. Now that there was more money, life was easier. Louis and Mary had a thatched house with a refrigerator in it. The old trucks had always been breaking down. Now, they could buy new trucks. They had plenty of gas and other supplies.

The camp was a lively place. Mary was constantly trailed by her five dogs. Other camp pets included a baboon, a crippled cat, and several foxes. A small antelope kept her two babies under Louis and Mary's bed. A pet monkey liked to rummage through unlocked suitcases. Oliver, a wildebeest calf, ran with the dogs. He often charged into a tent when someone was taking a bath. He liked to hear the bather scream and shout.

The cries of leopards, the shrieking of birds, and the barking of dogs filled the night air. Lions prowled the camp ground looking for food and water. Hyenas once broke into the refrigerator and ran off with the meat supply. Throwing firecrackers and banging pots drove away the wild animals for only a short time. One

Baboons play around Louis' Land Rover in Nairobi National Park. The Leakeys were able to buy new equipment and vehicles with the money Louis received from his lectures.

night, Mary saw eight leopards padding around her hut.[2]

The Zinj site was about ten feet above the bottom of the gorge. Above it, there was a steep cliff. Mary and her crew cut into the cliff for thirty feet. They then dug down through twenty feet of solid material.[3] The loose soil and rocks were removed with picks and shovels. Such tools could not be used on the living floor. Here only ice picks, dental picks, and small, soft brushes were used.[4]

Most of the crew had never worked for the Leakeys before. Mary expected them to be cautious and keen-eyed. She taught them to look for the chipped edge of a stone. She showed them how to sift the soil and pick out the tiniest bit of bone. They learned how to divide the site into four-foot squares. They removed the earth within each square in three-inch layers. Each fossil and artifact was left in place for Mary to number, map, and draw. All the loose soil was swept up, washed, and sieved.

Mary did not let her crew members talk or

Mary gives instructions to some crew members. She would teach her crew what to look for when sifting through the soil.

sing as they worked. "She knows that if you are talking, you do not see well," said one man. "This work was not easy. Everybody was working hard and studying hard."[5]

Mary swung a heavy pick along with her crew. She spent hours on her hands and knees, looking for "the merest gray speck against a brown background."[6] When she spotted one, she probed the spot with a dental pick, then brushed away the soil. Some of the workers did not like taking orders from a woman. They did not like Mary's harsh rules. A few of them left. The ones who stayed were grateful for the chance to learn so much.[7]

Mary also expected her sons to work hard. They repaired cars and trucks, tracked and shot game, helped to manage the camp, and built huts.

Jonathan's main interest was the study of snakes. But he also helped his brothers to excavate and catalog fossils and artifacts. Everyone's hard work paid off. Two hominid teeth and some skull fragments were found among some pebbles. Some of the fragments belonged to Zinj. Others were too thin to be a part of his skull. The teeth were too small. A short time later, a slender short leg bone was found. Louis said they may have belonged to a female Zinj. About a hundred yards away, in what was called Jonny's Site, Jonathan found the jawbone of a saber-toothed tiger. This animal had never before been found in East Africa.

After weeks of steady digging, Mary found a Zinj living floor. It was covered with thousands of fossils and tools. In one area, there were crushed animal bones. It was here that the hominids must have eaten their meals. They carved the raw meat from the bones. When the meat was gone, they smashed the bones to get the marrow.

Other scientists had believed that evidence of such ancient living floors had vanished, but Louis and Mary had believed that such sites would be found. Now, it was possible to see how early humans had lived.

Further digging uncovered a female hominid leg bone. In August 1960, Mary found fourteen foot bones. Together, they formed almost a complete foot. It was the first foot of an early bipedal hominid ever found. This ancient man had walked upright. Mary immediately telephoned Louis in Nairobi. He was so excited he drove 357 miles without stopping. During the next few days, he and Mary found several finger bones, a collarbone, and tiny bits of skull. All of these fossils were buried a foot below the Zinj living floor. This hominid must have been alive several thousand years before Zinj.

Meanwhile, Jonathan continued digging. In September 1960, he found two hominid skull fragments. They appeared to be from a child about eleven years old. Jonny's Child had lived 2 million years ago. He was different from Zinj. At that time, most scientists thought that different types of hominids had never lived alongside each other. Louis thought they were wrong.[8]

On November 2, Jonathan found a lower jaw with thirteen teeth. The front teeth were large, and the cheek teeth were small. Zinj had small front teeth and very large cheek teeth. Here was more proof that two types of ancient hominids had lived at the same time. The Leakeys had made another amazing discovery.

8

"Leakey's Luck"

BY THE END OF 1960, LOUIS AND MARY had enough money to hire all the helpers they needed. They could buy all the gasoline they needed. They did not have to stop work to raise money. Louis was now able to quit his job at the museum. He could spend more time digging for fossils. Mary was working at three different sites. At one site, she found a hominid toe bone. At another, she found the skeletons of an elephantlike creature, a giant antelope, and a giant porcupine.

Scientists from all over the world came to talk to Louis and Mary. Many of them visited their home in Nairobi. Guests did not have a quiet time there. Five dogs greeted them at the door. Hyraxes hid in the bathroom. An owl looked down from his nest on top of a cupboard. A monkey chattered from his perch on the couch. Tanks of tropical fish lined the walls. A cage of rattlesnakes lived next to the telephone. Whenever the phone rang, they rattled their tails.[1]

Jonathan's interest in snakes was evident in the front yard, where there were two pits. One held his pet python. His poisonous vipers lived in the other. In the backyard, there were small buildings where the workers lived with their families. Women cooked over open fires. Babies cried, and older children played.

Louis and Mary did not notice the noise and activity. They were too busy talking about their work. Louis was always making new plans. He wanted to study the African primates—the chimpanzees, orangutans, and gorillas. He wanted to explore new sites. He wanted to start a center for the study of African prehistory.

Louis did a lot of traveling. He went to Israel to explore a new digging site. He went to the United States to give lectures. He went to England to show Jonny's Child to several experts. He hoped they would agree that it was a *Homo*, a human.

Mary spent most of her time at Olduvai. The work day began at 7:00 A.M. At 1:00 P.M., everyone returned to camp for lunch. During the hot afternoons, newly found fossils and tools were sorted and recorded. After dinner, there were lively conversations among the visiting scientists.

Every day brought new discoveries. The crew uncovered a site where hominids had cut up an elephant. At the same time, twelve-year-old Philip found another living floor. It was almost 2 million years old.

Meanwhile, an expert named Phillip Tobias was studying the skull pieces of Jonny's Child. One main difference between apes and humans is brain size. Humans have larger brains than apes, so a human skull cavity is larger than an ape skull cavity. Tobias did not have a complete

*While digging at Olduvai Gorge, the Leakeys and their team found
many traces of ancient plants and animals. Louis shows off some of his
"precious finds." His hat contains a million-year-old elephant tooth.*

skull to study, so it was difficult for him to make exact measurements.

Louis waited impatiently for Tobias to finish his study. Someone else studied the leg, foot, and hand bones that had been found at the same site. The leg and foot bones were those of a bipedal being, one who stood upright on two feet. The hand bones were not the grasping hands of an ape, which swings from tree to tree. With its opposable thumb, this hand had a precision grip. Zinj had not made the tools in Bed One. This new species had made them.

For three years, Tobias studied the skull. The discovery of the hand and leg bones convinced him. "Once again, you have been proven right," he wrote to Louis. "This being was closer to being a *Homo* than to *Australopithecus*."[2]

Louis was thrilled. He named Jonny's Child *Homo habilis*, the "handyman." The world's first toolmaker had made anvils, awls, hammerstones, chisels, axes, and picks. He used both bones and stones to make his tools. Two million years earlier, he had shared the African plain

Louis shows a Homo habilis *jaw. Melvin Payne, of the National Geographic Society, holds a* Zinjanthropus (later, Australopithecus) *jaw. Note that the* Homo habilis *jaw is smaller and more delicate.*

with *Zinjanthropus*. Zinj had a smaller brain than *Homo habilis*. Zinj had not made tools. About 1 million years ago, Zinj had died out. *Homo habilis* had survived. It had become an ancestor of modern humans.

Louis knew that other scientists might not agree with him. His ideas were different from their ideas. But Louis had always liked a good argument.

Louis's excitement carried over to his other projects. He set up a center of African prehistory at the museum. He made a film about ancient art, fire-making, and tool-making. He raised money for the excavation in Israel. He also supported an excavation at Calico in Southern California. He hoped to prove that people had lived there more than fifty thousand years ago.

Louis trained a young woman named Jane Goodall to track and study wild animals. He then sent her to Gombe, Tanzania, where a group of chimpanzees lived. Jane watched the chimps eat. She watched them groom each other. She listened to their calls.

One day she saw a chimp pull the leaves off a twig. He pushed the twig into a termite nest, then pulled it out. The twig was covered with termites, which he ate. "I have seen the crude beginnings of tool-making," she wrote to Louis that night.

In 1967, Louis sent Dian Fossey to study Africa's mountain gorillas in Rwanda. Two years later, Dian wrote that the gorillas were tying and untying her shoelaces.

Later, Louis sent Biruté Galdikas to Indonesia, where she studied orangutans. He sent other young people to study the wildebeest and two different kinds of African monkeys.

Louis was now sixty-six years old. He was overweight. His teeth were decayed. Through the years, he suffered attacks of malaria and problems with his gall bladder. Sometimes he had severe headaches and epileptic seizures. He had painful arthritis in his hips. He could not walk far. He could no longer search for fossils.[3]

Louis's poor health did not cause him to slow down. One day in January 1970, he did not feel well. Still, he drove from Olduvai to Nairobi. He then boarded a plane and flew to London, where he had a heart attack, so he had to stay in bed for three weeks. During that time, visitors poured into his room. When he was alone, he made telephone calls and wrote letters.

His doctor told him he must remain calm. Louis could not follow his advice. He was upset because he could not oversee his projects.[4] He was upset because he had to cancel his lectures.[5] He was upset because Richard was making some changes at the museum.[6]

In July, Louis was able to return to Nairobi. In October, he flew to Calico. Volunteers had been digging there for six years. They had found some rocks that they thought might have been used as tools. They had also found a circle of rocks that could have been an ancient hearth.

These were the only results to come from a lot of hard work. A visit from Louis always cheered up the volunteers. "Dr. Leakey had a way of making even the littlest, most unimportant person feel important," said a member of the team. "He was so good to everybody."[7]

Louis was still certain that the Calico dig was important. He invited nearly a hundred scientists to see the objects the crew had found. Most of them believed that the "tools" were only rocks that had been tossed about by rushing water. They did not believe that the circle of rocks was a hearth. Louis asked them if they thought any of the rocks had been shaped by hominids. Many of the scientists said nothing. Some said "maybe" or "perhaps." They all liked Louis. They knew he had been sick. They did not want to upset him.[8]

Louis misunderstood the scientists' silence. He later told Mary, "It's all right; they all accepted the evidence." Mary did not argue with him. She knew he was wrong. The Calico rocks were only rocks. Louis had had many successes. Calico was one of his few failures. Everyone knew it except Louis.[9]

9

"An Unstoppable Man"

TO SUPPORT HIS MANY PROJECTS, LOUIS spent money as fast as it came in. Sometimes there was not enough money for Mary's work at Olduvai. She did not mind when Louis spent money on the Israeli dig. The team there had found tools and fossils that were more than a million years old. But Mary was upset when Louis kept spending money on the Calico project.[1]

Mary was also upset when Louis would not slow down. He traveled to France, England, and the United States to give lectures. Once he was so tired he collapsed. Later, he almost had another heart attack. His doctor told him to rest by the seashore. Here, he was attacked by a swarm of bees. Shouting for help, he hit his head on a wall and fell down.

By the time Louis was rescued, he had been stung hundreds of times. He suffered a stroke. For a week, he was paralyzed. He could not remember words and names. His recovery was slow. He hobbled about with a cane. His right arm was useless. Mary flew from Olduvai to see him.

"I'm just going to have to do less," he said to her. A minute later, he was planning a lecture tour.[2] In February 1971, he was released from the hospital. By April, he was in California. He had terrible headaches, but he kept traveling. In Los Angeles, he collapsed and was taken to a hospital. After an operation, his arm was only partly paralyzed. He had no more headaches. By the end of June, he was well enough to return to Africa. In September, he was off again to California.

Louis appeared to be "an unstoppable

man."[3] He gave lectures. He attended conferences. He helped students. He finished writing some books. He made plans for another expedition. To raise money, he went to Nairobi and London, then back to the United States. In his pocket, there was always a cast of an important find. Louis liked to surprise people by pulling it out.

Since Louis was away most of the time, Richard took his place at the museum. He also led his own expeditions. During the summer of 1972, his team was working on the shore of Lake Rudolf. They found pieces of a hominid skull in deposits that were 2.6 million years old. Some of the pieces were as small as a thumbnail. Richard's wife, Meave, put them together.

The completed skull was the largest early hominid skull that had ever been found. It was large enough to hold the brain of a *Homo erectus*, a man who stood upright.

The skull was named 1470, which was its field number. Richard could hardly wait to show it to his father. He had to hurry, because Louis was

In 1972, Richard discovered a humanlike skull (top) in the same deposit as an Australopithecus *skull.*

preparing to leave for London. Richard packed the skull in a wooden box. He and Mary flew to Nairobi.

They walked into Louis's office. Louis looked closely, then grinned. He had said that a large-brained *Homo* had walked the African plain more than 2 million years ago. Here at last was the proof he needed.

Louis looked up at his son. Their arguments were forgotten. "I give you 100 percent, Richard. I give you 100 percent."[4]

Louis, Mary, and Richard spent the rest of the day together. "Louis was excited, triumphant, sublimely happy," Mary later wrote.[5]

That night, Richard drove Louis to the airport. For some reason, he was worried about his father's trip. Richard told Louis to take care of himself.[6] Louis nodded. Then he boarded the plane.

The next day, Richard returned to Lake Rudolf. Mary drove back to Olduvai. On October 1, a plane landed there. Planes seldom came to Olduvai. When Philip stepped down from the cockpit, Mary knew that something had happened to Louis.

"Another heart attack?" she asked. "Or is he dead?"[7]

"Dead," Philip replied. He told her that Louis had arrived in London. Three days later, he collapsed and was rushed to the hospital. On October 1, at 9:30 A.M., he had died.

Louis's death was reported around the world. His funeral in Nairobi was attended by government officials and shopkeepers. White Kenyans and black Kenyans sat side by side. Louis's Kikuyu friends and famous scientists came to say good-bye. One speaker said that Louis had "courage, humor, determination, industry and humanity."[8]

Another said, "Louis was dedicated to pushing back the horizons of the past, no matter what the cost to his health."[9]

He had "an uncanny sense of knowing where fossils were to be found," said an anthropologist.[10]

"I still find it hard to realize that his

tremendous vitality and personality have gone," Mary wrote to a friend.[11]

A few days later, Mary and her sons returned to their busy lives. Richard was planning a trip abroad. Jonathan attended to his business, which was extracting snake venom for use in medicines. Philip went back to arranging safaris for tourists.

Louis's death changed Mary's life in one important way. She now had to give speeches and raise money. She had to become a world traveler. She went to the United States to give a series of lectures, and she went to scientific meetings. She attended the 1977 Pan-African Congress. She received medals and awards from universities and became used to the applause from her audiences.

Mary's happiest days were spent at Olduvai. Here she was "left in peace to . . . sort things out." She invited only a few people to visit her. Wild creatures and her dogs were her chosen companions. The dogs were trained not to chase the mice that took their biscuits. Birds came into

Louis and Mary Leakey cared for many orphaned wildebeest calves. After Louis Leakey passed away, Mary Leakey chose to keep dogs and wild creatures as her companions.

the camp for water and crumbs. Orphaned wildebeests slept in a grass hut next to her own hut.

Mary and her team continued their excavation of Beds Three and Four. In Beds One and Two, she had found *Homo habilis*. This species had used different parts of the gorge as campsites. They had lived beside freshwater streams that fed from a large lake. At first, their tools were simple choppers and small scrapers. Later, they had made heavier scrapers, awls, and handaxes.

Now Mary wanted to see how *Homo erectus* had lived. She had found *Homo erectus* fossils in Beds Three and Four. In the same area, she had found white quartzite handaxes with sharp tapering points. A mile away from the gorge, there was a large deposit of white quartzite. These hominids must have walked to this deposit to get material for their tools.

Mary's team also found an area in which there were hundreds of tools. Mingled with the tools were the bones of catfish, hippos, crocodiles, and a three-toed horse. The bones must have been the remains of *Homo erectus*'s meals. Later, in Bed Four, they found handaxes and cleavers made of lava. This volcanic rock probably came from a volcano located eight miles away. There were also many bone tools. One handaxe and a mortar were made from elephant bones.

All of these tools were found in or beside old streambeds. During the dry season, these hominids may have lived in the streambeds where they could dig for water.

Mary was puzzled when her team uncovered some deep pits in Bed Three. Some were three feet wide and a foot deep. Narrow channels connected the pits. Around their sides, there were scrapings that appeared to have been made by fingers. Mary had no idea what the hominids had been digging for.

"It's a bit difficult to get inside the mind of a *Homo erectus*," Mary said.[12] This mystery was added to her long list of unanswered questions.

10

Footprints from the Past

ONE AFTERNOON IN THE FALL OF 1974, Mary was examining the tools from Beds Three and Four. A visitor arrived in camp. He had found some animal fossils in a load of sand. The sand had come from Laetoli, which was thirty miles from Olduvai.

Mary decided to spend some time at Laetoli. By the end of the year, she and her team had found the fossils of thirteen hominids. It was later proved that these hominids had lived more than 3 million years earlier. Richard's fossil skull, 1470, was 2.6 million years old. Mary felt she may have found the world's oldest human

Workers sift soil in search of bone fragments at Olduvai.

ancestor. To prove it, she had to do some more excavating. If the fossils were from *Homo*, there might be some tools nearby.

By 1975, Mary and her team had found the remains of many new animal species. They had not found any more hominid fossils or any tools.

The following year, Mary moved to Laetoli. Philip directed the building of a new camp. Laetoli had its drawbacks. There were hundreds of poisonous snakes. It was infested with ticks. The buffaloes and elephants chased people. The nearest water hole was ten miles away. There were arguments among the team members.

Mary did not let any of these problems stop the work. Within a short time, the team had found hominid teeth and parts of a child's skeleton. They also found the footprints of an ancient elephant. The prints had been preserved in hardened volcanic ash. Along the elephant's trail, there were tracks of at least twenty other animals. The team had already found remains of many of these animals.

The volcanic ash preserved animal footprints.

Could it have preserved some hominid footprints too? In September, Philip and another crew member found what they thought was such a trail. The tracks looked as if they were made by a bipedal animal. They were short and wide. They included the imprint of a humanlike big toe.

Mary studied the prints for several months. She was still not sure they had been made by a hominid. This creature had walked with a "slow, rolling gait," like that of a bipedal chimpanzee.[1] To Mary, the prints did not appear to have been made by a creature who could chase game.

On July 27, two more footprints were found. These were different from the ones that had been found earlier. They looked almost the same as those of a modern human being. To Mary, the discovery was "immensely exciting, something extraordinary."[2] Here was proof that bipedalism had existed almost 3.5 million years ago.

The whole team went to work at the new site. Within a few days, they had uncovered two parallel hominid trails. It appeared that a light rain had been falling. Two hominids had walked across the plains. One was tall and one was short. During their walk, a nearby volcano had erupted. Ash covered the ground. The hominids' footprints were filled with ash and rainfall. The muddy ash later hardened and preserved the prints.

By September, Mary and her team had uncovered forty-seven hominid prints. It was a

The footprints found by Mary at Laetoli are thought to be 3.5 million years old. For the first time, there was evidence that human ancestors walked on two feet.

startling discovery. These prints were in sediment that was 3.6 million years old. Three-million-year-old hominid skulls were small. It had been thought that a large brain was the first difference between man and beast. It now appeared that a bipedal stride was the first difference.

The lack of tools at Laetoli told Mary something else. Bipedalism had occurred much earlier than tool-making. The first bipedal hominids did not have large brains. They were not intelligent enough to make tools.

The following year, two more footprint trails were uncovered. The trails were eighty feet long and very close together. Again, one hominid was taller than the other. His prints were very long. Two of those prints had double heel-prints. It appeared that there had been not two, but three hominids walking together. One was an adult male. A child had been walking beside him. A female had been behind the male. Her hands had probably been on his hips, so she had stepped directly into his prints.[3] Perhaps these footprints had been made by a family who had been frightened by the volcano's eruption and had clung to each other for protection.

The news of Mary's hominid trail flew around the world. "The footprints seem to have created rather a sensation," one scientist wrote. "Everyone is entranced!"

Another scientist called the prints "one of the most fascinating archaeological finds ever made."[4]

Mary herself said that the hominid trails were "perhaps the most remarkable find I have made in my whole career."[5]

She was joyful about her latest discoveries, but there was a cloud over her joy. Richard was very ill. His kidneys were failing. Without a new kidney, he would soon die. Philip, offered to donate one of his kidneys. The operation was a success.

Now Mary could again pay full attention to her work. She finished excavating at Laetoli. She still had found no tools there. Back in Olduvai, Mary wrote articles. She studied her fossils and artifacts. Sometimes she entertained visitors.

In 1977, Kenya and Tanzania, a neighboring

country, had a dispute. Tanzania closed its border. Mary's family could no longer come to see her. It was hard for her to get food and other supplies. Sometimes she did not get her mail. Life at Olduvai became very difficult.

One afternoon in November 1982, Mary was alone in camp. She took a nap. When she awoke, she found she was blind in her left eye. The next day she flew to Nairobi to see a doctor. He told her that she would never see out of that eye again.

The news made Mary very sad, but Richard's pep talks cheered her up. Mary was now seventy years old. She had spent most of her life searching for humankind's ancestors. Now, her main fieldwork was done. It was time to write up the results. It was time to leave Olduvai.

In May 1983, Mary closed up her little hut at the gorge. She had lived there for almost twenty years. She had seen floods and droughts. She had coped with invasions of snakes and grasshoppers. She had fought off prowling lions. She had seen leopards and rhinoceroses disappear from the gorge. Hunters had thinned out the herds of wild animals.

Mary moved to the house that she and Louis had built near Nairobi. Here, there was no danger from wild creatures, and there was plenty of water. Louis's books, journals, medals, and pictures surrounded her. She could spend her time writing books and articles. She could see her sons and their wives and children. She could go to meetings and visit with other scientists.

Mary Leakey died on December 9, 1996. She and Louis had traced human history from over 3 million years ago to five hundred thousand years ago. But that history is still filled with gaps. Richard helped to fill in some of those gaps. Now he is busy trying to save Kenya's wildlife from hunters and disease. His daughter, Louise, directs her own fossil-hunting expeditions.

Richard's wife, Meave, has been hunting fossils for many years. In the summer of 1995, she and her team discovered another species of bipedal hominid. This hominid lived 4 million years ago. It was walking upright almost five hundred thousand years before Mary's Laetoli footprints were made.

The work that Louis and Mary Leakey began is being continued by members of their family. Their discoveries help us to learn about our ancestors. And the more we learn about our ancestors, the more we will understand ourselves.

Meave and Richard examine a skull they discovered in 1972. Meave has become the new leader of the Leakey family's work. She made headlines in 1995, when her team discovered the 4 million year old jaw of a new hominid species, Australopithecus anamensis.

Activities

Make Your Own Dig

Materials needed:

- a tub or sturdy box about two feet across and a foot deep

- pieces of a broken pottery dish or jar
- other objects such as: a bracelet, dried fruit, paper clip, nail, nut, safety pin, pair of tweezers, small screwdriver, piece of macaroni, coin, arm or leg from a broken doll, wheel from a toy car

- an old strainer or a large piece of screen

- an old towel

Procedure:

While you are away, have someone place two or three objects in the bottom of the container.

Cover them with a four-inch layer of dirt. Add the remaining objects and cover them.

Now, the dig is ready for you to excavate. First, using string, divide the top layer of dirt into four equal sections. Using a teaspoon and a small paintbrush, carefully remove three inches of dirt from one section. Put the dirt to one side. Place the uncovered objects, or artifacts, on the towel. Using the strainer, sift through the dirt to make certain you found all the objects. In the same way, excavate the other three sections.

Using the same method, excavate the second layer, or bed, then the third.

Studying Artifacts

Materials needed:

- Your excavated artifacts

Procedure:

Pretend that you have never seen these objects before. Write the answers to the following questions about each one.

(A) What material is the artifact made of?

(B) How do you think it was made? (Was it molded, fired, pressed, or chipped?)

(C) What decorations are on the object?

(D) Describe the shape of the object.

(E) What was the object used for?

(F) If the artifact is part of something larger, estimate the size and/or shape of the complete object.

(G) Glue the pieces of the broken jar or dish together.

Discovering Your Own Roots

Procedure:

Write the answers to the following questions in a notebook.

(A) What is your ethnic background?

(B) Where were you born?

(C) Where were your parents born?

(D) Where were your grandparents born?

(E) What holidays does your family celebrate?

(F) What are your family's favorite foods?

(G) What sports does your family like?

(H) What type of music does your family like?

(I) How is your life different from your parents' lives when they were your age?

Make Your Own Cave Paintings

Materials:

- four large paper grocery bags
- colored chalk or tempra paints
- a book with pictures of prehistoric animals and people (You can find one in a library.)

Procedure:

Dampen the bags, and then crumple them up. Then carefully smooth out the crumpled bags. Let the bags dry. They will now resemble the rough rock walls of a cave. Now copy some of the pictures in the book onto the "cave wall."

Important Discoveries of Human Origins

Millions of Years Ago	Leakey Family Expedition Finds	Other Finds
Today		
		Neanderthal Man, *Homo neanderthalensis,* (1856)
.5		
		"Peking Man," *Homo erectus,* (W.C. Pei, 1928–37)
1		"Java Man," *Homo erectus,* (Eugène Dubois, 1891)
	"Turkana Boy," *Homo erectus* (Kimoya Kimeu, expedition led by Richard Leakey, 1984)	
1.5	"Jonny's Child," *Homo habilis* (Jonathan Leakey, 1960)	
	"Zinj," *Australopithecus boisei* (Mary D. Leakey, 1959)	
2	1470, *Homo rudolfensis* (Bernard Ngeneo, expedition led by Richard Leakey, 1972)	
2.5		Taung Child, *Australopithecus africanus* (M. de Bruyn, expedition led by Raymond Dart, 1924)
3		"Lucy," *Australopithecus afarensis* (Donald Johanson, 1974)
3.5	Laetoli Footprints *A. afarensis* (Maundu Muluila; expedition led by Mary Leakey, 1974)	
4	*Australopithecus anamensis* (Peter Nzube; expedition led by Meave Leakey, 1994)	

Chronology

1856—First Neanderthal skulls are found.

1891—First *Homo erectus* skulls found in Java, [Indonesia].

1903—Louis Seymour Bazett Leakey was born on August 7, in Kenya.

1913—Mary Douglas Nicol was born on February 6, in London.

1919—The Leakeys return to England.

1922—Louis enters Cambridge University.

1924—First *Australopithecus africanus* skulls found at Taung, South Africa.

1926—Mary Nicol and her mother move back to London; Louis graduates from Cambridge.

1927—Louis begins first expedition in Kenya.

1928—Louis marries Wilfrida "Frida" Avern.

1931—Louis's daughter, Priscilla, is born.

1932—Louis begins his exploration at Kanam and Olduvai; Louis travels to London and meets Mary Nicol.

1933—Louis's son, Colin, is born.

1935—Percy Boswell returns to Kanam with Louis.

1936—Louis and Frida are divorced in October; Louis and Mary are married on December 24, in Ware, England.

1940—Son Jonathan born, November 4; Great Britain enters World War II.

1943—Baby daughter, Deborah, dies.

1944—Son Richard is born on December 19.

1945—World War II ends.

1948—Mary discovers skull of *Proconsul africanus*

1949—Philip was born on June 21, 1949.

1959—Discovered skull of *Zinjanthropus boisei* (later *Australopithecus boisei*).

1960—Louis sends Jane Goodall to study chimpanzees in Tanzania; discovery of Jonny's Child.

1961—Tanzania gains independence.

1963—Kenya gains independence; discovery of *Homo habilis*.

1966—Richard marries Margaret Cropper.

1967—Louis sends Dian Fosse to study the mountain gorilla in Rwanda.

1969—Louis sends Birute Galdikas to Indonesia to study the orangutans; birth of Richard's daughter, Anna, in March; Richard and Margaret divorce.

1970—Louis suffers heart attack; Richard marries Meave Epps.

1972—Richard discovers 2.6 million-year-old Homo skull at Lake Turkana; Louis dies on October 1, in London.

1973—Birth of Louise, Richard and Meave's daughter in March.

1974—Discovery of "Lucy" (*Australopithecus afarensis*) by Donald Johanson; birth of Samira, Richard and Meave's second daughter on June 12.

1978—Mary discovers Laetoli footprints.

1984—Mary publishes autobiography, *Disclosing the Past*; discovery of Turkana Boy, at Lake Turkana by Leakey Team.

1994—Meave Leakey's team discovers 4 million-year-old *Australopithecus anamensis* in Ethiopia.

1996—Mary Leakey dies on December 9.

Chapter Notes

Chapter 1

1. Sonia Cole, *Leakey's Luck* (New York: Harcourt Brace Jovanovich, 1975), p. 30.

2. Ibid., p. 38.

3. Ibid., p. 42.

4. Ibid., p. 38.

5. Mary Leakey, *Disclosing the Past* (Garden City, N.Y., Doubleday, 1984), p. 25.

6. Ibid., p. 29.

7. Ibid., p. 32.

Chapter 2

1. Roger Lewin, *Bones of Contention* (New York: Simon and Schuster, 1987), p. 134.

2. Virginia Morell, *Ancestral Passions* (New York: Simon and Schuster, 1995), p. 38.

3. Sonia Cole, *Leakey's Luck* (New York: Harcourt Brace Jovanovich, 1975), p. 69.

4. Morell, p. 46.

5. Ibid., p. 139.

6. Ibid., p. 58.

7. Robert Silverberg, *Man Before Adam* (Philadelphia: Macrae Smith Company, 1964), p. 173.

8. Morell, p. 61.

9. Cole, p. 91.

10. Ibid., p. 91.

11. Lewin, p. 131.

12. Cole, p. 100.

Chapter 3

1. Mary Leakey, *Disclosing the Past* (Garden City, N.Y.: Doubleday, 1984), p. 45.

2. Virginia Morell, *Ancestral Passions* (New York: Simon and Schuster, 1995), p. 83.

3. Ibid., p. 89.

4. Ibid, p. 96.

5. Leakey, p. 63.

6. Morell, p. 101.

7. Leakey, p. 59.

8. Sonia Cole, *Leakey's Luck* (New York: Harcourt Brace Jovanovich, 1975), p. 122.

9. Morell, p. 113.

10. Leakey, p. 71.

11. Ibid.

Chapter 4

1. Mary Leakey, *Disclosing the Past* (Garden City, N.Y.: Doubleday, 1984), P. 80.

2. Sonia Cole, *Leakey's Luck* (New York: Harcourt Brace Jovanovich, 1975), p. 142.

3. Virginia Morell, *Ancestral Passions* (New York: Simon and Schuster, 1995), p. 126.

4. Ibid., p. 178.

5. Leakey, p. 89.

6. Morell, p. 138.

7. Ibid.

8. Ibid., p. 139.

9. Ibid., p. 142.

Chapter 5

1. Richard Leakey, *One Life* (Salem, N.H.: Salem Publishing House, 1983), p. 24.

2. Mary Leakey, *Disclosing the Past* (Garden City, N.Y.: Doubleday, 1984), p. 98.

3. Ibid., p. 99.

4. Virginia Morell, *Ancestral Passions* (New York, Simon and Schuster, 1995), p. 157.

5. Sonia Cole, *Leakey's Luck* (New York: Harcourt Brace Jovanovich, 1975), p. 175.

6. Mary Leakey, p. 99.

7. Morell, p. 154.

8. Mary Leakey, p. 100.

9. Richard Leakey, p. 28.

Chapter 6

1. Mary Leakey, *Disclosing the Past* (Garden City, N.Y.: Doubleday, 1984), p. 112.

2. Virginia Morell, *Ancestral Passions* (New York: Simon and Schuster, 1995), p. 172.

3. Ibid.

4. Ibid.

5. Ibid., p. 178.

6. Sonia Cole, *Leakey's Luck* (New York: Harcourt Brace Jovanovich, 1975), p. 218.

7. Morell, p. 158.

8. Ibid., p. 178.

9. Ibid., p. 162.

10. Richard Leakey, *One Life* (Salem, N.H.: Salem Publishing House, 1983), p. 24.

11. Mary Leakey, p. 121.

12. Robert Silverberg, *Man Before Adam* (Philadelphia: Macrae Smith Company, 1964), p. 176.

13. Mary Leakey, p. 121.

14. Cole, p. 231.

Chapter 7

1. Virginia Morell, *Ancestral Passions* (New York: Simon and Schuster, 1995), p. 193.

2. Ibid., p. 222.

3. Ibid., p. 199.

4. Ibid., p. 200.

5. Ibid., p. 201.

6. Robert Silverberg, *Man Before Adam* (Philadelphia: Macrae Smith Company, 1964), p. 175.

7. Morell, p. 201.

8. Ibid., p. 206.

Chapter 8

1. Mary Leakey, *Disclosing the Past* (Garden City, N.Y.: Doubleday, 1984), p. 117.

2. Virginia Morell, *Ancestral Passions* (New York: Simon and Schuster, 1995), p. 234.

3. Sonia Cole, *Leakey's Luck* (New York: Harcourt Brace Jovanovich, 1975), p. 79.

4. Morell, p. 372.

5. Cole, p. 369.

6. Morell, p. 361.

7. Ibid., p. 363.

8. Leakey, p. 143.

9. Ibid., p. 144.

Chapter 9

1. Mary Leakey, *Disclosing the Past* (Garden City, N.Y., Doubleday, 1984), p. 144.

2. Virginia Morell, Ancestral Passions (New York: Simon and Schuster, 1995), p. 371.

3. Ibid., p. 381.

4. Ibid., p. 400.

5. Mary Leakey, p. 159.

6. Richard Leakey, *One Life* (Salem, N.H.: Salem Publishing House, 1983), p. 150.

7. Morell, p. 401.

8. Sonia Cole, *Leakey's Luck* (New York: Harcourt Brace Jovanovich, 1975), p. 408.

9. Ibid.

10. Ibid.

11. Morell, p. 404.

12. Ibid., p. 442.

Chapter 10

1. Virginia Morell, *Ancestral Passions* (New York: Simon and Schuster, 1995), p. 371.

2. Mary Leakey, *Disclosing the Past* (Garden City, N.Y.: Doubleday, 1984), p. 177.

3. Ibid., p. 178.

4. Morell, p. 499.

5. Roger Lewin, *Bones of Contention* (New York: Simon and Schuster, 1987), p. 150.

Glossary

anthropology—The study of human beings. There are two branches, physical anthropology, which is the study of the physical characteristics of human beings, including evolution, and cultural anthropology, which is the study of human cultures and societies.

archaeology—The study of ancient human cultures.

artifact—An ancient object made or crafted by humans.

australopithecine—The name given to a group of humanlike creatures that lived between 8 and 2 million years ago.

Australopithecus boisei—An early hominid that lived in East Africa about 2 million years ago. This is the same species as that discovered by the Leakeys at Olduvai Gorge in 1959 and originally named *Zinjanthropus boisei*.

choppers—Primitive stone tools used by ancient hominids to rip meat from bones.

excavation—In archaeology and anthropology, the systematic uncovering of a historic or prehistoric site.

fossils—The remains of prehistoric life forms.

geology—The study of the earth.

Great Rift Valley—A huge gap in the earth's crust that stretches from the African nation of Mozambique to the Sea of Galilee in Israel. The rift is caused by the shifting of two of the earth's plates.

handaxe—An all-purpose double-edged cutting tool used by ancient human beings.

hominids—Animals that are similar or closely related to human beings. All are extinct.

Homo erectus—An intermediate ancestor of human beings that became extinct approximately 250,000 years ago. Though their skulls were smaller, the rest of the skeleton is similar to present-day humans.

Homo habilis—An early hominid that lived approximately 1.75 million years ago and is believed to have been a toolmaker.

Homo sapiens—Modern human beings (*Homo sapiens sapiens*), including Neanderthals (*Homo sapiens neanderthalis*).

Kikuyu—An East African people who are the largest ethnic group in Kenya.

malaria—A sometimes fatal disease carried by mosquitoes in tropical climates.

Mau Mau—A group founded in the 1950s by the Kikuyu in Kenya, seeking independence from Great Britain. Kenya became independent in 1963.

Miocene—In geologic time, the period beginning approximately 24 million years ago and ending about 5 million years ago.

Olduvai Gorge—Part of the Great Rift Valley, this thirty-mile-long ravine in northern Tanzania is the site of many important discoveries in the study of human evolution.

prehistory—The study of events prior to recorded human history.

primates—The mammal family that includes lemurs, apes, and humans. Unlike other mammals, most primates can grasp objects with their hands or feet, and most have forward-facing (stereoscopic) eyes, which gives them the ability to judge depth.

Proconsul—A genus of apelike creatures that lived approximately 25 million years ago, and are thought to have been the ancestors of modern apes and humans.

scrapers—Stone tools used by ancient human beings to remove flesh from bone.

Stone Age—The name prehistorians give to the period of human existence from the first use of tools until about 10,000 years ago.

Zinjanthropus boisei—The name first given by the Leakeys to the species now known as *Australopithecus boisei*.

Further Reading

Badone, Donalda. *Time Detectives: Clues from our Past*. Buffalo: Firefly Books, 1996.

Blauer, Ettagale and Jason Laure. *Tanzania*. Chicago: Children's Press, 1994

Diagram Group Staff and David Lambert. *The Field Guide to Early Man*. New York: Facts on File, 1988.

Facchini, Fiorenzo. Rocco Serini, trans. *Humans*. Chatham, N.J.: Raintree, 1994.

Johanson, Donald. *From Lucy to Language*. New York: Simon & Schuster, 1996.

Lewin, Roger. *The Origin of Modern Humans: A Scientific American Library Volume*. New York: Scientific American Books for Young Readers, 1995.

Ng'Weno, Fleur. *Kenya*. North Pomfret, Vt.: Trafalgar Square, 1992.

Index